Emotions

Janet West

BookLeaf Publishing
India | USA | UK

Presentation by *BookLeaf Publishing*

Web: www.bookleafpub.com

E-mail: info@bookleafpub.com

ISBN : 978-93-5744-308-1

First edition 2022

DEDICATION

To Laurie and my Queen much love

ACKNOWLEDGEMENT

To my family who have been my inspiration

PREFACE

Thanks for looking I hope you enjoy my squiggles

Our Life

Although we were so very young
I've loved you from the start
On the very day we met
You walked off with my heart
We used to talk for hours
Planning out our life
All the things that we would do
Once I became your wife
Sometimes I wish we could go back
Take a different path
One that's not so rocky
One to make us laugh
I know we had our ups and downs
Sometimes we'd just despair
I want you to know for sure
My love is forever there.

Friends

When life seems to get you down and you feel
all alone
I want you to remember I won't leave you on
your own
Although the miles may part us, the time goes
by so fast
Just close your eyes remember my promise of
the past
I think of you most everyday and wonder how
you do
Always and forever my friend I will be there for
you

Marriage

Here's hoping that the journey you've started
will be fun
The knot you've tied together will never be
undone
The love and laughter on your way will make
you more secure
We hope the love you feel right now will be
forever more.

Sunshine

As the sun shines on the flowers
I sit and watch for hours and hours
People rushing to and fro
To their destinations they go
I watch the birds and the children play
The sun shining down
What a beautiful day

Granddaughter 18th

On the day that you were born
My heart was filled with love
You were sent to us a special gift
From the angels up above
I watched you walk
I watched you grow
I hold the moments in my heart
Now a beautiful young lady
I knew you'd be right from the start
Now that you have reached eighteen
Another chapter comes along
I know you'll step up to the mark
Surviving with a song
I am so very proud of you
You're stronger than you know
 I'll forever be your anchor
 I will never let you go.

Infinity and beyond.

Birthday milestone 40

We can't believe you are 40
How the times fly by
So many years and memories
Passed in the wink of an eye
We hope your day is a happy one
Your presents plentiful too
We're sending love and happiness
Especially for you.

Son

On the day that you were born
They laid you in my arms
I was instantly won over
With your eyes and all your charms
Then was time to watch you grow
Be with you through the years
Joining in your laughter
Wiping up your tears
Now that you are fully grown
Gone off on your own
Know I'll always be right here
My house always your home.

My dad

As I sit and watch a while
For all the things that bring a smile
Children playing happily
So unaware of what's to be
I think of you and all the years
The crazy laughter heartfelt tears
A lifetime gone passed by so fast
No more future just the past
But oh what memories we made
To always be and never fade
So as I sit and watch a while
I have so much to make me smile

War

Why are they always fighting
What are they fighting for
All of this endless bloodshed
This terrible thing called war
Blood flowing like a river
Tears streaming like the rain
Why are they always fighting
Will there ever be peace again.

Remembrance

As time goes by and life goes on
My love for you keeps me strong
A saddened smile, a silent tear
Treasured memories hold you near
The lessons and love you gave to me
I'll keep in my heart eternally

Love

As you start your journey as a happy loving pair
I hope the years bring joy to you
With love beyond compare
You'll always have each other
Your vows made from the heart
Here's wishing all the years will be
As loving as the start

Loss

A troubled soul now peaceful
A young life gone too soon
I know you'll be there shinning
A bright star with the moon
A son, a brother, an uncle
We pray you're now at rest
You'll never be forgotten
Now you're up there with the best

The Boss

The boss here is a cheerful soul
A happy smile for all
So she deserves this poem
To hang upon her wall
Both staff and customers alike
Are served with cheerful tact
Manageress of the year
Is due here that's a fact

The Fight

You are an inspiration a lesson to us all
The way you keep on fighting
Though your backs against the wall
You smile and put a brave face on
Though you're crying deep inside
The way you cope with everything
Should fill you up with pride
I pray that you can beat these ails
That life has thrown at you
I wish you joy and happiness
For the rest of your life too.

My mum

My heart still hurts, my eyes still cry
Since we had to say goodbye
I wish that you were here with me
To heal these wounds no one can see
I love you mum and miss you so
It's so unfair you had to go
Life goes on, time will heal
Always mum I'll love you still

Grandson

On the day that you were born
The angels up above
Sent us a precious grandson
To fill our hearts with love
As I looked upon your face
My heart just filled with joy
I know just how lucky we are
To have this perfect boy

Daughters

I am the luckiest mum in the world
To have two beautiful girls
I cherish every moment
We have shared throughout the years
I am so proud of all the things that you have
both achieved
I wish you love and happiness with everything
you need
My love is always there for you my home an
open door
Nothing stops the way I feel now and forever
more.

Loneliness

As I lie here in my bed
Thoughts spinning round inside my head
Thoughts of my life and how I lived
The people I loved, the ones I forgive
My tears run freely down my face
I wonder how I got to this place
My heart is breaking piece by piece
If only I could make this heartache cease
I try each day to start anew
Try happy Thoughts to get me through
But the Thoughts just keep spinning in my head
My heart keeps on feeling like a piece of lead.

www.ingramcontent.com/pod-product-compliance
Lightning Source LLC
LaVergne TN
LVHW050300200726
843509LV00015B/3081